Tools for Problem Solving

Level F

STECK-VAUGHN
COMPANY

A Division of Harcourt Brace & Company

Acknowledgments

Executive Editor	Diane Sharpe
Senior Project Editor	Donna Rodgers
Editor	Allison Welch
Design Project Manager	Sheryl Cota
Cover Design	John Harrison
Electronic Production	PC&F, Inc.

Photography Cover: ©W.P. Fleming/Viesti Associates; p.4 ©David Barnes/The Stock Market; p.5 ©PhotoDisc; p.5 ©Robert Brenner/PhotoEdit; pp.8, 9 (t), 10 (t) ©PhotoDisc; p.12 ©Michael Newman/PhotoEdit; p.14 (m) ©PhotoDisc; p.14 (b) ©Tom McCarthy/PhotoEdit; pp.15 (b), 17 (t) ©PhotoDisc; p.19 ©Tony Duffy/NBC/Allsport; p.20 ©David Young-Wolfe/PhotoEdit; p.22 ©David Young-Wolfe/PhotoEdit; p.24 ©Vic Bider/PhotoEdit; p.25 ©Robert E. Daemmrich/Tony Stone Images; p.26 ©Johathan Nourok/PhotoEdit; p.27 ©Jose Carrillo/PhotoEdit; pp.28 (t), 29 (m), 32 (t), 37 (t) ©PhotoDisc; p.38 ©E.R. Degginger/Earth Scenes; pp.39 (b), 41 (t) ©PhotoDisc; p.41 (b) ©Wallace Kirkland/Animals Animals; pp.44 (t), 49, 50(b) ©PhotoDisc; p.54 (t) Corel Photo Studios; p.54 (b) ©PhotoDisc; p.55 ©Dick Young/Unicorn Stock Photos; pp.58, 59, 60, 62 (l), 66 ©PhotoDisc; p.70 (b) ©Michael Newman/PhotoEdit; p.80 ©PhotoDisc; p.84 (t) ©Superstock; pp.84 (m, b), 85 (t) ©PhotoDisc; p.85 (b) Corel Photo Studios; pp.86, 87 (m), 90 (t,b) ©PhotoDisc; p.90 (m) ©Superstock; p.91 (t) ©Michael Newman/PhotoEdit; p.94 (t) ©Reed/Williams/Animals Animals; pp.94 (m), 96 (b) ©PhotoDisc; Additional photography by Digital Studios.

Illustration pp.6, 7, 11, 12, 16, 30, 31, 45, 63, 67, 68, 69, 75, 78, 79, 81, 82, 88 Dave Blanchette.

ISBN 0-8172-8130-4

Contents

Unit 1: **What a Deal!** 4
Strategies: Choose the Operation,
Solve Multi-Step Problems
Skills: Mixed Operations, Percent

Unit 2: **Sports Stats!** 18
Strategies: Make a Graph,
Make an Organized List
Skill: Analyzing Data

Review: **Units 1–2** 32

Unit 3: **Treasure Boxes** 34
Strategies: Make a Model, Use a Formula
Skills: Volume and Surface Area

Unit 4: **Code Breakers** 48
Strategies: Guess and Check,
Solve Multi-Step Problems
Skills: Exponents and Square Roots

Review: **Units 3–4** 62

Unit 5: **Games and Contests** 64
Strategies: Make a Tree Diagram,
Make a Table
Skills: Data and Probability

Unit 6: **At the Mall** 78
Strategies: Use Logical Reasoning,
Work Backward
Skills: Comparing Data, Venn Diagrams

Review: **Units 5–6** 92

Final Review 94

What a Deal!

Lesson 1   Write a Plan

Justin, Gino, Kim, and Melissa are planning to go to an amusement park. The normal admission price is $23.95 each, but on Wednesdays the bargain price is $18.80 each. If the group of friends goes to the park on a Wednesday, how much in all will their tickets cost?

Write a plan to solve the problem.

Step 1   Write in your own words what you need to find out.

_____

_____

Step 2   Write the facts that will be useful.

_____

_____

Step 3   Explain or show how you will solve the problem.

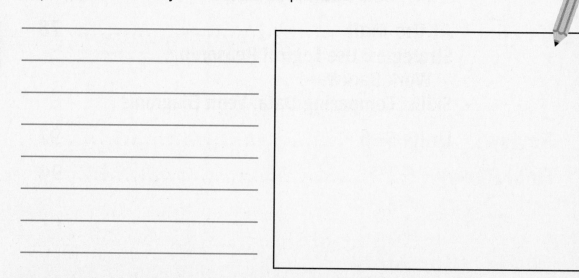

_____

_____

_____

_____

_____

_____

Choose the Operation

Try choosing the operation to solve the problem.

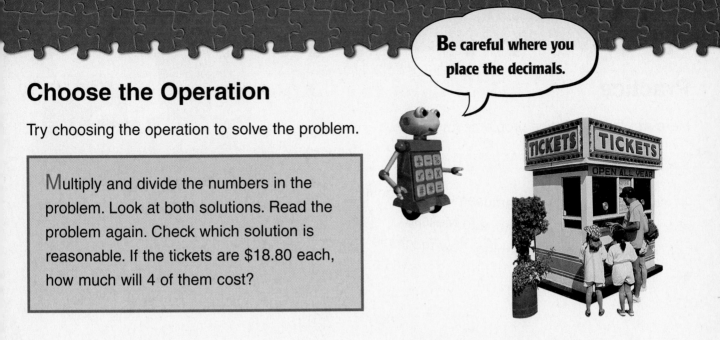

Multiply and divide the numbers in the problem. Look at both solutions. Read the problem again. Check which solution is reasonable. If the tickets are $18.80 each, how much will 4 of them cost?

1. If you multiply, what answer do you get?

$18.80
× 4

2. If you divide, what answer do you get?

4)$18.80

3. Read the problem again. Does the answer make more sense when you multiply or when you divide? How do you know?

_____

_____

4. Can you solve the problem by adding? Explain how it might be done.

_____

_____

5. How much would 4 tickets cost at the regular price of $23.95 each? How much do the friends save in all by going to the amusement park on a Wednesday?

Practice

Here are three practice problems for you.

Quick-Solve 1
Kim's lunch in the amusement park cost $6.14. If Justin, Gino, and Melissa ordered the same thing, how much did 4 lunches cost?

Quick-Solve 2
Gino bought 4 snow cones for himself and his friends. The snow cones were $1.45 each. How much did Gino pay in all?

Quick-Solve 3
To play Laser Tag in the amusement park, Gino, Kim, Melissa, and Justin had to pay $3.95 each. They were also joined by 2 other friends. How much did 6 tickets cost?

Applying Strategies

Use What You Know

At the amusement park, there is a recording studio where you can make your own audio cassette or video tape. Justin and Gino decide to sing a country song on a video. If they share the cost equally, how much will each of them pay for one video?

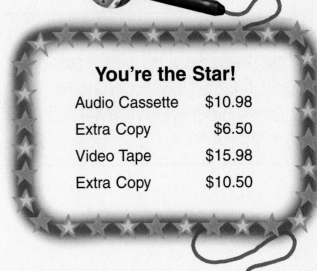

You're the Star!

Audio Cassette	$10.98
Extra Copy	$6.50
Video Tape	$15.98
Extra Copy	$10.50

Multiply and divide the numbers in the problem. Try to decide which solution is reasonable.

1. If you multiply, what answer do you get?

$$\begin{array}{r} \$15.98 \\ \times \quad 2 \\ \hline \end{array}$$

2. If you divide, what answer do you get?

$$2\overline{)\$15.98}$$

3. Read the problem again. Does the answer make more sense when you multiply or when you divide? How do you know?

_____

_____

4. What if Justin and Gino each want a copy of the video tape? How much would it cost for one video and one copy? If they share the cost equally, what will each of them pay?

_____

_____

Lesson 2   Write a Plan

Cosby Music Store is having a sale on CDs. Everything in the store is 30% off! Gail's favorite CD is usually $15.99. How much can she save by buying it during the sale?

Write a plan to solve the problem.

Step 1

Write in your own words what you need to find out.

_____

_____

_____

Step 2

Write the facts that will be useful.

_____

_____

_____

Step 3

Explain or show how you will solve the problem.

_____

_____

_____

_____

_____

_____

_____

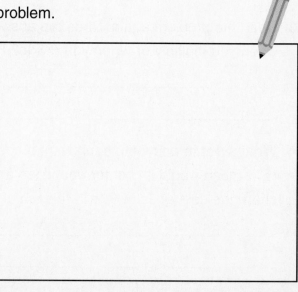

Choose the Operation

Try choosing the operation to solve the problem.

Change the percent to a decimal before you begin.
30% = 0.30

> Multiply and divide the numbers in the problem. Will 30% of $15.99 be greater than or less than $15.99? How much can Gail save by buying the CD during the sale?

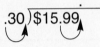

1. If you multiply, what answer do you get?

$15.99
×   .30

2. If you divide, what answer do you get?

.30)$15.99

3. Read the problem again. Is 30% of $15.99 greater than or less than $15.99?

_____

4. Does the answer make more sense when you multiply or when you divide? How much can Gail save? Round the answer to the nearest cent. Explain.

_____

_____

5. You have found the amount that Gail can save. Now find how much she will pay for the CD at the sale price. Explain or show how you solve the problem.

Practice

Here are three practice problems for you.

Quick-Solve 1

A camera store is having a 50% off sale. If the regular price of a camera is $172.80, what is the sale price?

Quick-Solve 2

The camera store is also selling picture frames for 40% off. Emil buys a frame that usually costs $22.00. How much can he save by buying it during the sale?

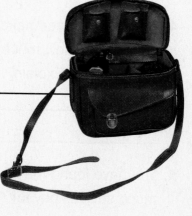

Quick-Solve 3

Susan finds a camera bag that usually costs $35.20. She gets it during the sale for 75% of that price. What did she pay for the camera bag?

Applying Strategies

Use What You Know

If you need help, look back to pages 8 and 9.

Miss Hill paid $352.30 for a washing machine during a sale. She got it for 65% of the original price. What was the original price of the washing machine?

1. If you multiply, what answer do you get?

$$\begin{array}{r} \$352.30 \\ \times \quad .65 \\ \hline \end{array}$$

2. If you divide, what answer do you get?

$$.65\overline{)\$352.30}$$

3. Read the problem again. Is the original price of the washing machine greater than or less than $352.30?

_____

4. Does the answer make more sense when you multiply or when you divide? What was the original price of the washing machine? Explain how you know.

_____

_____

5. Miss Hill also bought a dryer during the sale. She paid $280.00 plus tax. The sales tax was 8%. How much tax did she pay? Hint: 8% = 0.08.

Lesson 3 Solve Multi-Step Problems

You know how to choose the operation to solve problems.
Now try solving a multi-step problem.

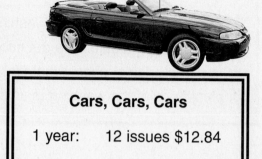

Heather and Keiko are selling magazines for a
school project. They tell Evan that he can save
money by getting his favorite car magazine for two
years. How much will Evan save per magazine at
the 2-year price instead of the 1-year price?

Cars, Cars, Cars		
1 year:	12 issues	$12.84
2 years:	24 issues	$19.92

1. If Evan orders the magazine for 1 year,
   what is the cost for each magazine?

2. If Evan orders the magazine for 2 years,
   what is the cost for each magazine?

3. Find the difference between the cost
   per magazine for 1 year and the cost per
   magazine for 2 years. How much will
   Evan save per magazine?

4. The store price for the magazine is $2.95 for
   each monthly issue. How much can Evan
   save on 12 issues if he places a 1-year order
   instead of paying the store price?

Practice

Here are three practice problems for you.

Quick-Solve 1

William's favorite socks cost $3.69 a pair. They also come in packages of 3 pairs for $10.00. How much can William save on 3 pairs of socks by buying the package?

Quick-Solve 2

Tiffany is saving money to buy a pair of ice skates which cost $76.46. She has already saved $32.71. If she saves $6.25 each week, in how many weeks will she have enough money to buy the skates?

Quick-Solve 3

Otto, Neil, and Tara want to go to a concert that costs $17.50 per ticket. Together they have saved $50.00. How much more money do they need?

Use What You Know

Now try solving multi-step problems that involve percent.

Mr. Garza buys a computer for $1,850.00. He gets a special deal with no interest for 6 months. He pays 15% down and plans to pay off the computer in 5 months. If he makes 5 equal monthly payments, how much will each payment be?

Remember:
15% = 0.15

1. How much is the down payment?

2. How much does Mr. Garza still owe after the down payment?

3. After the down payment, Mr. Garza makes 5 equal monthly payments. How much is each payment?

4. What if Mr. Garza pays 25% down on the computer? How much less would his monthly payments be then?

5. Mr. Garza sees a sign on a printer that says, "Regular price $288.00. Special sale 20% off." What is the sale price of the printer?

Solving Multi-Step Problems: Percent

Lesson 4 Solve It Your Way

Read each problem and decide how you will find the solution.

You may want to choose one of these strategies for each problem.

Choose the Operation
Solve Multi-Step Problems

1. A nylon dog leash costs $12.79. A leather leash the same length costs $23.99. How much will you save by buying the nylon leash?

2. Karen buys a dog house for $152.10. She also buys a dog heater for $45.90. The sales tax is 6%. How much does she pay in all? Hint: 6% = 0.06.

3. A dog bed is regularly priced at $38.20. How much can you save with a 20% off coupon? What would be the price of the dog bed with the coupon?

4. Suppose you feed your dog two cans of dog food each day. One can of dog food costs $0.89. How much will you spend on dog food each week?

5. A box of 24 dog bones costs $6.48. A bag of 56 dog bones costs $13.44. Which is the better buy? How do you know?

6. Carl buys 2 pet toys that cost $3.65 each and a dog door for $19.70. Tax on his purchase is 8%. What is his total bill?

Practice

Now write your own multi-step problems.

Quick-Solve 1

The answer to a problem is "$310.00." What might the question be? Write your own problem to share with a friend. If your friend does not get an answer of $310.00, discuss how you might change the problem or the solution to match.

Quick-Solve 2

The answer to a problem is "25%." What might the question be? Write your own problem to share with a friend. If your friend does not get an answer of 25%, discuss how you might change the problem or the solution to match.

Quick-Solve 3

The answer to a problem is "20% off." What might the question be? Write your own problem to share with a friend. If your friend does not get an answer of 20% off, discuss how you might change the problem or the solution to match.

Review Show What You Know

Work in a small group. Suppose you are placing an order for art supplies from this advertisement.

WATERCOLORS		MARKERS		DRAWING PADS		BRUSHES	
10-tube set	$23.90	each	$1.90	9 × 12	$5.80	$\frac{1}{16}$-inch	$0.60
12-tube set	$28.92	set of 3	$5.50	12 × 18	$7.60	$\frac{1}{8}$-inch	$0.72

1. Which is a better buy, a 10-tube set of watercolors or a 12-tube set? Explain.

   _____

2. How much can you save if you buy the set of three markers rather than buying each marker separately?

   _____

3. Suppose you have $50.00 to spend on art supplies. Decide what to buy. Fill in the order form. Add your item totals, find the tax amount, and add shipping to find the order total.

ORDER FORM			
Item	**Description**	**Quantity**	**Total**
		Item Total	
		6% Tax	
		Shipping	$5.95
		Total	

UNIT 2 Sports Stats!

Lesson 1   Write a Plan

An Olympic swimmer's goal is to swim the 50-meter freestyle in 45 seconds. The calendar shows her best time for each day of swimming practice. Based on the data her coach collected, will her time be 45 seconds by the January 23 meet?

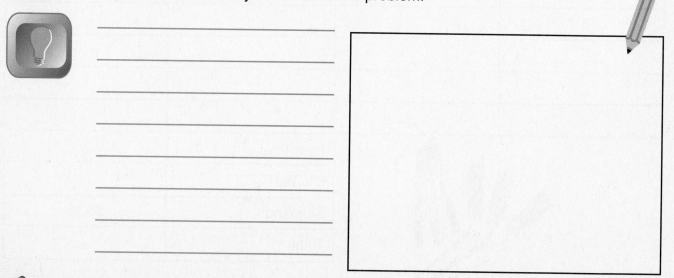

January						
Sun	Mon	Tue	Wed	Thu	Fri	Sat
	⊿ Practice Schedule			1	2	3
4	5 Practice 57 sec. 1	6	7 Practice 54 sec. 2	8	9 Practice 52 sec. 3	10
11	12 Practice 51 sec. 4	13	14 Practice 49 sec. 5	15	16 Practice 49 sec. 6	17
18	19 Practice 48 sec. 7	20	21 Practice 8	22	23 First Meet	24
25	26 Practice 9	27	28 Practice 10	29	30 Practice 11	31

Write a plan to solve the problem.

Step 1   Write in your own words what you need to find out.

_____

_____

Step 2   Write the facts that will be useful.

_____

_____

Step 3   Explain or show how you will solve the problem.

_____

_____

_____

_____

_____

_____

_____

Writing a Plan: Analyzing Data

Make a Graph

Try making a bar graph to solve the problem.

Look at the swim times shown on the calendar. The times shown are rounded to the nearest second. Draw the bars on the graph to show the times for each practice session. Then analyze the data. Based on the data, will her time be 45 seconds by the January 23 meet?

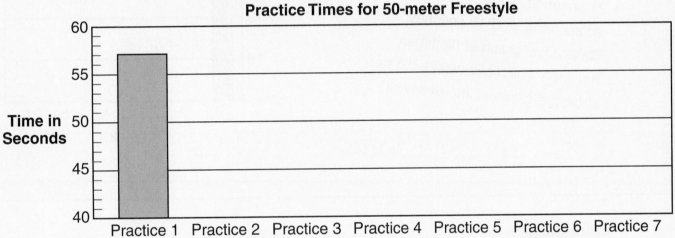

Practice Times for 50-meter Freestyle

1. About how much did her time change between Practice 2 and Practice 3?

2. About how much slower is her time at Practice 7 than the 45-second goal?

3. By what amount of time does the swimmer's time decrease at each practice? How much did her time decrease over this period of time?

4. If her time decreases as much between Practice 7 and the Meet as it did between Practice 1 and Practice 3, will she reach her 45-second goal? What if her time decreases at the same rate as it did between Practice 5 and Practice 7. Will she meet her goal then?

Making a Graph: Analyzing Data

Practice

Here are three practice problems for you.

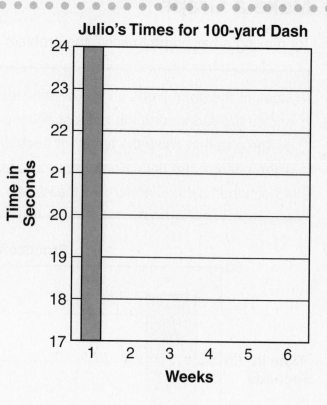

Julio's Times for 100-yard Dash

(bar graph with y-axis "Time in Seconds" from 17 to 24, x-axis "Weeks" from 1 to 6)

Quick-Solve 1

Julio wants to break the sixth grade record for the 100-yard dash. Each week he records his best time. For the first six weeks, his best times are 24 seconds, 22 seconds, 21 seconds, 20 seconds, 20 seconds, and 19 seconds. Make a bar graph of his times. Between which two weeks did he show the greatest improvement?

Quick-Solve 2

Using the graph you made above, what was the difference in Julio's times between Week 1 and Week 3? What was the difference between Week 4 and Week 6?

Quick-Solve 3

If the sixth grade record for the 100-yard dash is 17 seconds and Julio continues to improve as much as he did between Week 5 and Week 6, how many more weeks will he need before he can tie the school record?

Applying Strategies

Use What You Know

The coach of the Yankees baseball team wants to give an award to the player whose batting average has improved the most over the past five years. Compare the batting averages of Tino Martinez and Luis Sojo. Who will receive the award?

Year	Tino Martinez	Luis Sojo
Year 1	.27	.17
Year 2	.26	.28
Year 3	.29	.29
Year 4	.29	.22
Year 5	.30	.31

Use the data from the table to make a double bar graph of each player's batting averages. Be sure to follow the key for each player. Then use the graph to answer the questions.

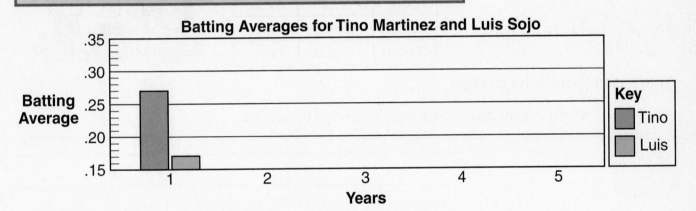

1. Between which two years did Tino's batting average increase the most? Between which two years did Luis's average increase the most?

_____

2. During which two years were Tino's averages closest? During which two years were Luis's averages closest?

_____

3. What was the overall increase in batting average for the five-year period for Tino? What was the increase for Luis?

_____

4. Who will receive the award for the most improved batting average? How do you know?

_____

Making a Graph: Analyzing Data

Lesson 2 Write a Plan

Suppose you found these statistics for the starting players on your favorite women's basketball team. What is the **mean** height? What is the **median** height? What height is the **mode?**

Mean is the average of the numbers in a set of data. *Median* is the middle number. *Mode* is the number that occurs most often. There may be more than one mode.

Wolverines Basketball Team		
Player	**Position**	**Height**
Hobbs	Forward	73 in.
King	Forward	72 in.
Kruk	Center	74 in.
Clark	Guard	69 in.
Brown	Guard	69 in.
Cash	Guard	68 in.
Toore	Forward	72 in.
Truman	Center	74 in.
Gaston	Guard	69 in.

Write a plan to solve the problem.

Step 1 Write in your own words what you need to find out.

_____

_____

Step 2 Write the facts that will be useful.

_____

_____

Step 3 Explain or show how you will solve the problem.

_____

_____

_____

_____

_____

_____

_____

Writing a Plan: Analyzing Data

Make a Graph

Try making a graph to solve the problem.

Wolverines Basketball Team		
Player	**Position**	**Height**
Hobbs	Forward	73 in.
King	Forward	72 in.
Kruk	Center	74 in.
Clark	Guard	69 in.
Brown	Guard	69 in.
Cash	Guard	68 in.
Toore	Forward	72 in.
Truman	Center	74 in.
Gaston	Guard	69 in.

> Use the list of heights to complete the frequency graph below. What is the **mean** height? What is the **median** height? What height is the **mode?**

1. Complete the frequency graph. Look at the list of heights for the players. For each player, draw an X above her height in the frequency graph.

Wolverines Basketball Team

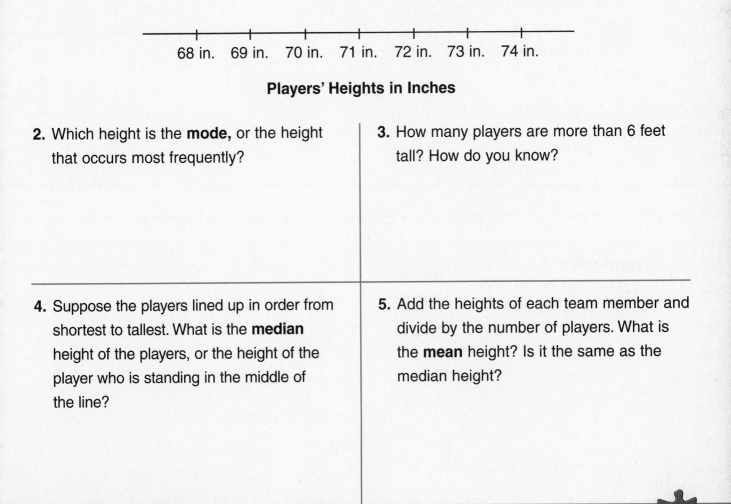

68 in. 69 in. 70 in. 71 in. 72 in. 73 in. 74 in.

Players' Heights in Inches

2. Which height is the **mode,** or the height that occurs most frequently?

3. How many players are more than 6 feet tall? How do you know?

4. Suppose the players lined up in order from shortest to tallest. What is the **median** height of the players, or the height of the player who is standing in the middle of the line?

5. Add the heights of each team member and divide by the number of players. What is the **mean** height? Is it the same as the median height?

Practice

Here are three practice problems for you.

Quick-Solve 1

The ages of the members of the Comets basketball team are: 29, 26, 27, 33, 25, 27, 23, 25, 31, and 24. Make a frequency graph of the team members' ages. Which is the mean age?

Ages of the Comets Players

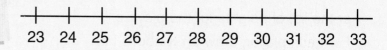

23 24 25 26 27 28 29 30 31 32 33

Quick-Solve 2

What is the mode (or modes) for the team members' ages? Remember, there can be more than one mode in a given set of data.

Quick-Solve 3

What is the median age of the Comets players? Is the median the same as the mean?

Use What You Know

For a class trip, Teresa's class went to a miniature golf course. What was the mean, median, and mode scores for the class?

Fill in the remaining scores on the frequency graph. Then use the list of scores to complete the graph. Draw an X for each score. Use the graph to analyze the data.

Miniature Golf Scores

35	32	38	37	40	37	35
38	34	41	42	39	44	34
44	38	40	34	38	37	41

Students' Golf Scores

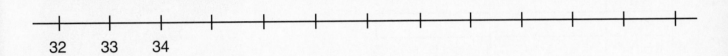

32   33   34

1. How many students played miniature golf? How did you find the answer?

2. What is the mean score?

3. What is the mode of the golf scores? How many students played this score?

4. Teresa scored a 38. Is her score the same as the median score? How do you know?

Lesson 3   Make an Organized List

You have made graphs to analyze data.
Now try making an organized list to solve a problem.

Snowboarding Slalom	
Name	Time (seconds)
Lopez	54.29
Loveless	51.83
Esposito	51.77
Wecker	55.53
McNeil	54.91
Clark	58.37
Shuwei	62.65
Perkins	59.93
Yong	64.21
Novak	70.11

The judge at a snowboarding competition records the slalom times of the top ten snowboarders who complete the course. In which place did each snowboarder finish?

1. List the snowboarders in order from fastest to slowest times in the table below. Remember that the fastest time is the lowest number.

Snowboarding Finalists		
Place	Name	Time (seconds)
1st		
2nd		
3rd		
4th		
5th		
6th		
7th		
8th		
9th		
10th		

2. Which snowboarder will win the first-place trophy? _____

3. The top three finalists will compete in the national competition.

   What is the mean time of the top three finalists? _____

4. In order to qualify for the state competition next year, all snowboarders must have a slalom time below the median time for this year's competition. What time must each snowboarder make in order to compete next year?
   Hint: If there are two middle numbers, the median is the average of

   the two numbers. _____

Making an Organized List: Analyzing Data

Practice

Here are three practice problems for you.

The table shows the times for the top five finishers in a 10-mile mountain bike race. List the riders from fastest to slowest.

Rider	Time (Hours: Min.)	Rider	Time (Hours: Min.)
Brewer	1:34		
Riley	1:22		
Edgar	1:16		
Worley	1:29		
Ingram	1:29		
Owens	1:19		
Rankin	1:28		

Quick-Solve 1

The three riders with the fastest times will race in the next round of the competition. Who are they?

Quick-Solve 2

What rider's time represents the median time?

Quick-Solve 3

Find the fastest and the slowest times on your list. What is the mean of these two numbers? Is the mean greater than or less than the median time for all seven riders? Hint: Convert each time to minutes in order to find the mean.

Use What You Know

The table shows the salaries of the pitchers on a major league baseball team. What is the median salary of a pitcher on this team? What salary represents the mode?

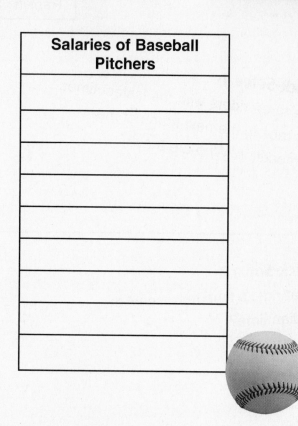

List the salaries in order from greatest to least to complete the table. Then analyze the data.

Salaries of Baseball Pitchers
$2,675,000
$500,000
$750,000
$528,000
$1,500,000
$320,000
$130,000
$270,000
$320,000

Salaries of Baseball Pitchers

1. What is the difference between the greatest and the least salary? _____

2. What is the median salary? _____

3. What salary is the mode? _____

4. Suppose the pitchers with the two highest salaries left the team. The two new pitchers each earn $350,000. What is the median salary of pitchers on this

   team now? _____

Making an Organized List: Analyzing Data

Lesson 4 Solve It Your Way

Read each problem and decide how you will find the solution.

You may want to choose one of these strategies for each problem.

Make a Graph
Make an Organized List

1. The weights of each member of a school's wrestling team are 125, 215, 135, 103, 112, 153, 160, 189, 140, 245, and 174 pounds. What is the median weight of the team members? What is the mean weight of the team?

Make a graph or organized list here.

2. In the first 6 games of the season, the Thrashers soccer team made the following scores against their opponents: 3 to 2, 4 to 1, 2 to 2, 7 to 5, 3 to 6, and 1 to 1. In which game did the Thrashers win by the most points? Who scored the most points in a single game, the Thrashers or their opponents?

3. A group of 8 friends went bowling and recorded the number of strikes they made: Nick–2, Nori–4, Sue–3, Franz–4, Jake–2, Carla–6, Daniel–4, Sylvia–5. What is the median number of strikes the friends made? What is the mode for the number of strikes?

4. In their last game of the season, the Lions completed passes for the following yards: 4, 12, 7, 8, 25, 8, 14, 12, 21, 6. Calculate the median, mode, and mean for the number of yards.

Practice

Now write your own problems.

| The Rolling Spoke | | | |
| Mountain Bike Sales | | 10-Speed Sales | |
Quarter of Year	Bikes Sold	Quarter of Year	10-Speeds Sold
1st Quarter Jan.–Mar.	50	1st Quarter Jan.–Mar.	75
2nd Quarter Apr.–Jun.	150	2nd Quarter Apr.–Jun.	50
3rd Quarter Jul.–Sept.	75	3rd Quarter Jul.–Sept.	60
4th Quarter Oct.–Dec.	25	4th Quarter Oct.–Dec.	40

Quick-Solve 1

The answer to a problem is "The mean is 75." What might the question be? Write your own problem to share with a friend. If your friend does not get a mean of 75, discuss how you might change the problem or the solution to match.

Quick-Solve 2

The answer to a problem is "The difference is 100." What might the question be? Write your own problem to share with a friend. If your friend does not get a difference of 100, discuss how you might change the problem or the solution to match.

Quick-Solve 3

The answer to a problem is "The sum is 65." What might the question be? Write your own problem to share with a friend. If your friend does not get a sum of 65, discuss how you might change the problem or the solution to match.

Applying Strategies

Review Show What You Know

Work in a small group. Conduct a survey of the classmates in your group. Make a table showing the month in which each student was born.

1. Make a table to show your data.

Name	Month Born

2. Make a frequency graph of your data. In which month(s) were most students born? In other words, what month represents the mode?

3. In which month were the fewest students born?

_____

4. What month represents the median? _____

5. Draw a bar graph of your data. Is this a good way to show the information? Why or why not?

Review   Units 1–2

Read each problem and decide how you will find the solution.

Wow! You can choose from all these strategies!

**Choose the Operation
Solve Multi-Step Problems
Make a Graph
Make an Organized List**

1. Vicki and her sister want to buy their favorite CD for $15.98. If they share the cost, how much will each of them pay?

2. Chad bought a baseball bat on sale for 60% off the regular price. The regular price was $28.80. How much money did Chad save?

3. Seven runners trained for a benefit race. They ran the following miles in the first week of their training: 6, 3, 5, 4, 3, 8, 5. What is the median number of miles they ran? What number or numbers represent the mode?

4. Yolanda bought her mother a flower vase priced at $17.50. Sales tax was 8%. What was the total cost of the vase?

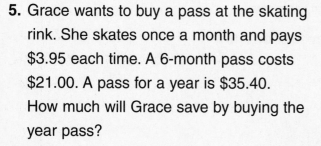

5. Grace wants to buy a pass at the skating rink. She skates once a month and pays $3.95 each time. A 6-month pass costs $21.00. A pass for a year is $35.40. How much will Grace save by buying the year pass?

6. The distances for the top five record holders in the high school women's shot put event were 40, 38, 34, 37, and 38 feet. What is the mean distance?

7. Over the past 10 years, new players have joined the Fancy Feet Soccer League. Eight new players joined the first year, then 12, 19, 7, 22, 15, 24, 9, 20, and 17 the following years. Complete the bar graph. The greatest increase in players occurred between which two years?

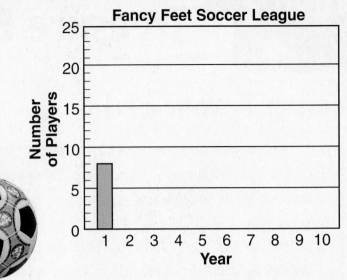

Fancy Feet Soccer League

Number of Players (y-axis: 0, 5, 10, 15, 20, 25)

Year (x-axis: 1 2 3 4 5 6 7 8 9 10)

8. The greatest decrease in players occurred between which two years?

9. What is the mean number of new players joining the league each year?

10. Each year, Coach Davis buys special colored shoelaces for the new players in the league. He receives a 5% discount if he buys 10 to 19 pairs of laces, and a 10% discount if he buys 20 or more. If the laces normally cost $1.20 per pair, how much will Coach Davis pay for laces in the year in which the most new players joined?

11. Over the past 10 years, which discount (10% off, 5% off, or no discount at all) has Coach Davis received most often? How do you know?

UNIT 3   Treasure Boxes

Lesson 1   Write a Plan

Ana has a set of 3 boxes for keeping her special treasures. Each box is a perfectly square cube. The largest measures 5 centimeters on all sides. The next box has sides of 4 centimeters. The smallest box is a 3-centimeter cube. For fun, Ana stacks the boxes as a tower with the largest on bottom and the smallest on top. What is the volume of Ana's treasure tower?

Write a plan to solve the problem.

Step 1   Write in your own words what you need to find out.

_____

_____

Step 2   Write the facts that will be useful.

_____

_____

Step 3   Explain or show how you will solve the problem.

_____

_____

_____

_____

_____

_____

_____

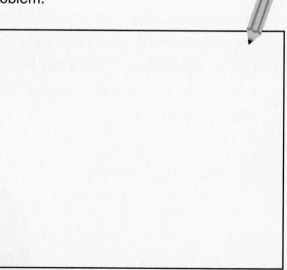

Make a Model

Try making a model with centimeter cubes to solve the problem.

> Find the volume of each box in Ana's tower. Then add them together to find the volume of the treasure tower.

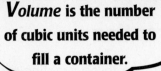

Volume is the number of cubic units needed to fill a container.

1. Stack centimeter cubes to represent the box that is 3 cm wide, 3 cm long, and 3 cm high. Fill the middle with cubes as well. How many centimeter cubes does it take? Write your answer as a number of cubic centimeters. You may write *cu cm* or *cm³*.

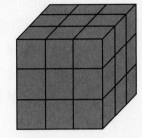

2. Now do the same with centimeter cubes to build the next box. For the 4-cm box, begin with a flat layer that is 4 cm wide, 4 cm long, and has all the inside cubes filled in. Then build the other layers to make the model 4 cm high. How many cubic centimeters will fill a box that is a 4-cm cube?

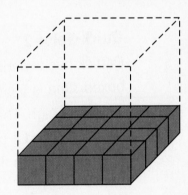

3. Build a model with centimeter cubes that is 5 cm wide, 5 cm long, and 5 cm high. Make sure all the inside cubes are also filled in. How many cubic centimeters will fill a box that is a 5-cm cube?

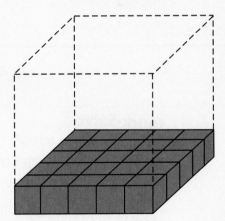

4. Add the volume of the three boxes. What is the total volume of Ana's treasure tower? Write your answer as a number of cubic centimeters.

Practice

Here are three practice problems for you.

Quick-Solve 1

Margot makes her own miniature treasure boxes. The smallest box is a 1-centimeter cube. The next box is 2 cm by 2 cm by 2 cm. The third box is 3 cm by 3 cm by 3 cm. If Margot stacks these in a tower, what is the volume of her tower?

Quick-Solve 2

Patrick has two miniature treasure boxes. One is 5 cm wide, 5 cm long, and 2 cm high. The other is 3 cm wide, 4 cm long, and 4 cm high. Which treasure box has the greater volume?

Quick-Solve 3

Jeffrey has two miniature boxes. The volume of the smaller box is half the volume of the larger box. The larger box is a 4-cm cube with a volume of 64. Can the smaller box be a cube? Explain why or why not.

Use What You Know

If you need help, look back to pages 34 and 35.

Mark collects fly-fishing baits. He keeps them in a large box. The top tray is divided into 5 compartments. The dimensions of each compartment are 5 cm by 5 cm by 4 cm. What is the volume of the top tray of the box?

1. Make a model of one compartment that is 5 centimeters wide, 5 centimeters long, and 4 centimeters high. Fill the middle with cubes as well. How many centimeter cubes does it take? What is the volume of one compartment?

_____

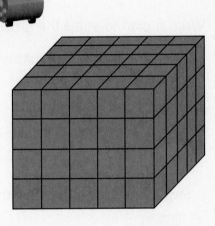

2. How many compartments are there in the

top tray? _____

3. What is the volume of the top tray in Mark's bait box?

_____

4. The top tray lifts out to reveal a compartment that is 25 centimeters long, 20 centimeters wide, and 4 centimeters high. Make a model or draw a picture to find the volume of the large compartment.

5. What is the total volume of the bait box?

_____

Lesson 2   Write a Plan

Nathan collects fossils. He has a special coral that he keeps in a box lined with acid-free paper. The box is 5 cm long, 3 cm wide, and 3 cm high. What is the surface area of the acid-free paper?

Write a plan to solve the problem.

Step 1

Write in your own words what you need to find out.

_____

_____

_____

Step 2

Write the facts that will be useful.

_____

_____

_____

Step 3

Explain or show how you will solve the problem.

Writing a Plan: Surface Area

Make a Model

Try making a model to solve the problem.

Surface area is the sum of the areas of the faces of a solid figure.

> Make a model of the box using graph paper or dot paper. Make sure that your box is 5 cm long, 3 cm wide, and 3 cm high. Find the area of each face of the box. Add them together to find the total surface area. The flat box has been drawn for you.

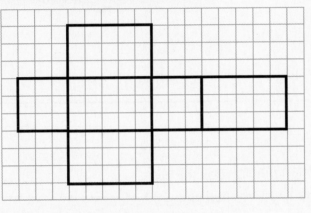

1. Look at the drawing of the flat box. How does it help you to understand the meaning of *surface area*?

_____

2. To find area, multiply length × width. Four faces of the box have a length of 5 cm and a width of 3 cm. What is the area of each of these faces? The answer in square centimeters can be written as *sq cm* or as *cm²*. _____

3. The other two faces of the box have a length of 3 cm and a width of 3 cm. What is the area of each of these faces? _____

4. What is the surface area of the acid-free paper that lines this box? Explain the steps you use to find the answer. Hint: Make sure you count all six faces.

_____

_____

Practice

Here are three practice problems for you.

Quick-Solve 1

Liliana still has the first tooth she ever lost in a little box. The height of the box is 2 cm. The length and width are 4 cm. She covered the box with colorful paper. What is the surface area of the paper?

Quick-Solve 2

Fred made a wooden display box for his baseball trophy. He lined the five sides of the open box with mirror tiles. The box is 12 inches high, 6 inches long, and 4 inches wide. The open front is 12 inches by 6 inches. What is the surface area of the tiles?

Quick-Solve 3

Jonathan keeps his Trilobite fossil in a cube-shaped box that has a volume of 64 cubic cm. The box is lined with felt to protect the fossil from scratching. What is the surface area covered with felt?

Applying Strategies

Use What You Know

Michael loves insects. He found a dead firefly in the backyard and decided to keep it. His mom helped him cut pieces of plexiglass which he glued together to make a case. The dimensions of the case are 8 cm by 6 cm by 5 cm. What is the surface area of the plexiglass used?

If you need help, look back to pages 8 and 9.

1. Make a model of the rectangular prism using graph paper. Draw the box flat before you begin. Three sides have been done for you below.

2. Find the area of each face of the rectangular prism. Add them together. What is the surface area of the plexiglass

   Michael used? _____

3. What would the surface area be if one of the 6 cm by

   8 cm faces was removed? _____

Lesson 3   Use a Formula

You have made models to solve problems.
Now try using a formula.

Remember:
Area = Length × Width.
Surface area is the sum
of all the faces.

Hanna bought a special box to hold her shell collection. She lined the entire box with velvet. The dimensions of the box are 30 cm, 10 cm, and 8 cm. What is the surface area of the velvet?

Opposite sides of a rectangular prism are the same size. Suppose we call the ends of the box A and B, the front and back C and D, and the top and bottom E and F.

E

A

C

10 cm

8 cm

30 cm

1. What are the dimensions of faces A and B? _____

2. What are the dimensions of faces C and D? _____

3. What are the dimensions of faces E and F? _____

4. Use a formula to find the area of each face.

Face	Length × Width	Area
A	×	cm²
B	×	cm²
C	×	cm²
D	×	cm²
E	×	cm²
F	×	cm²

5. What is the surface area of the velvet? _____ cm²

Using a Formula: Surface Area

Practice

Here are three practice problems for you.

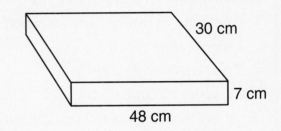

Quick-Solve 1

Kapil keeps his newspaper clippings of sports events in a shirt box. He covered the lid of the box with newspaper. The dimensions of the box lid are 48 cm, 30 cm, and 7 cm. What is the surface area covered with newsprint? Hint: There are only 5 sides.

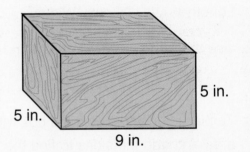

Quick-Solve 2

Carla has a wooden keepsake box that is 9 inches long and 5 inches wide. It is 5 inches tall. Each surface is lined with red felt. What is the surface area of the red felt?

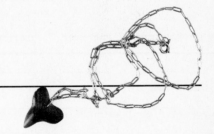

Quick-Solve 3

Louis made a cardboard box for his shark tooth. The bottom of the box is 2 inches wide and 2 inches long. The total surface area of the cardboard is 24 sq in. Draw the box flat.

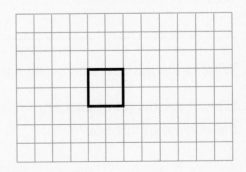

Use What You Know

You learned how to use a formula to find surface area.

Now try using a formula to find volume.

> Zachary built an open box for his coin collection.
> He used the following pieces of wood:
>   1 piece: 15 cm by 8 cm
>   2 pieces: 8 cm by 5 cm
>   2 pieces: 15 cm by 5 cm.
> What is the volume of the box Zachary built?

Remember:
Volume = Length × Width × Height

1. Look at the drawing of Zachary's box. Write the length, width, and height.

Length = _____ cm   Width = _____ cm   Height = _____cm

8 cm

5 cm

15 cm

2. Use the formula for volume to find the volume of the box.

_____ × _____ × _____ = _____

3. Zachary decided to line his box with felt. Use the formula for area and add the sides to find the surface area of the lining. Hint: Remember that there is no lid, so there are not 6 sides.

_____ × _____ = _____

_____ × _____ = _____

_____ × _____ = _____

_____ × _____ = _____

_____ × _____ = _____

4. What is the surface area of the lining? _____

5. What if the height of Zachary's box was 6 cm? What would be the volume of this box?

_____ × _____ × _____ = _____

Lesson 4 Solve It Your Way

Read each problem and decide how you will find the solution.

You may choose one of these strategies for each problem.

Make a Model
Use a Formula

1. The library at Jackson Middle School has a large collection of CD-ROMs. They are in long cases that measure 30 cm long, 14 cm wide, and 15 cm high. What is the volume of one case?

2. Johnson Treasure Store received a shipping box of 12 model train engines. Each engine came in a smaller box that was a 4-inch cube. Which shipping box below could they have been in?

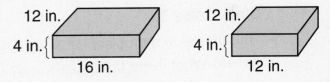

12 in. 4 in. 16 in.

12 in. 4 in. 12 in.

3. Abraham made a round clay bowl for his mother. It was 20 cm in diameter and 12 cm in height. He put it in a box that was 21 cm wide, 21 cm long, and 12 cm high. What was the volume of the box?

4. Box A is 5 cm long and 4 cm wide. Box B is 10 cm long and 3 cm wide. Both boxes have a volume of 120 square centimeters. Which box has the greater height? How do you know?

Practice

Now write your own problems using volume and surface area.

Quick-Solve 1

The answer to a problem is "64 cubic centimeters." What might the question be? Write your own problem to share with a friend. If your friend does not get an answer of 64 cm³, discuss how you might change the problem or the solution to match.

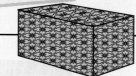

Quick-Solve 2

The answer to a problem is "24 square inches." What might the question be? Write your own problem to share with a friend. If your friend does not get an answer of 24 in.², discuss how you might change the problem or the solution to match.

Quick-Solve 3

The answer to a problem is "90 cubic inches." What might the question be? Write your own problem to share with a friend. If your friend does not get an answer of 90 in.³, discuss how you might change the problem or the solution to match.

Applying Strategies

Review Show What You Know

Work in a small group.

When a rectangular prism is drawn flat, the drawing is called a *net*. One of the drawings below is a net. The other cannot be folded to make a box, so it is not a net. Figure out which one is a net. Then draw your own net.

1. Copy the drawing, cut it out, and try to fold it into a box. Is it a net? Write *yes* or *no*.

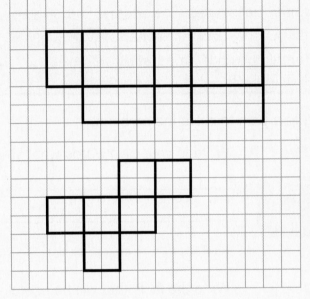

2. Copy the drawing, cut it out, and try to fold it into a box. Is it a net? Write *yes* or *no*.

3. Use the graph paper below to draw your own net. Then test it by copying it, cutting it out, and folding it into a box. Finally, find the surface area and volume of your box. Use the squares on the graph paper as units.

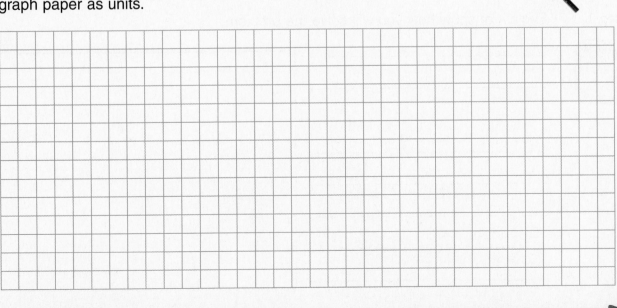

Code Breakers

Lesson 1 Write a Plan

Keenan sent party invitations to all of his math classmates. The address was written as a code. Look at Keenan's invitation, break the code, and find his address.

You're Invited

What: Keenan's Math Party

When: Saturday at 2:00

Where: $7^3 + 4$ Avenue D

See you there if you

know your exponents!

Write a plan to solve the problem.

Step 1

Write in your own words what you need to find out.

_____

_____

_____

Step 2

Write the facts that will be useful.

_____

_____

_____

Step 3

Explain or show how you will solve the problem.

_____

_____

_____

_____

_____

_____

_____

Guess and Check

An *exponent* tells you how many times to use the base number as a factor.
$$7^3 = 7 \times 7 \times 7$$

Try guessing and checking to solve the problem.

Keenan wrote his address as $7^3 + 4$. Several of his friends made guesses to calculate his house number. Look at their guesses and find the one that you think is the closest. Then check your solution.

1. Rebecca rounded 7 to 10. Her guess was $10^3 + 4$. What was Rebecca's guess? Is it greater than or less than Keenan's house number?

2. Brad has the solution to 5^3 memorized. He guessed $5^3 + 4$. What was Brad's guess? Is it greater than or less than Keenan's house number?

3. Sarah knew that $7 \times 7 = 49$. She rounded 49 to 50 and multiplied by 7. Then she added 4. What was Sarah's guess? Is it greater than or less than Keenan's address?

4. Is Rebecca's, Brad's, or Sarah's guess closest to Keenan's house number? How do you know?

5. Break the code! What is Keenan's house number? Explain how you know that your solution is reasonable.

Practice

Here are three practice problems for you.

Quick-Solve 1

Keenan has a jar of jelly beans at the math party. He asks everyone to guess how many jelly beans are in the jar. Erika guesses 200, SuChin guesses 194, and Kevin guesses 190. The actual number is equal to 14^2. Whose guess is closest?

Quick-Solve 2

Tomás worked for his uncle for $3 the first day. Each day that followed, he earned 3 times the previous day's pay. How much did he earn on the fifth day? Write the number of dollars in exponent form.

Quick-Solve 3

Tomás used part of his earnings to bring food to Keenan's math party. He spent a number of dollars equal to 2^4. Keenan paid him back with a $20 bill. Was that too much, too little, or just right?

Use What You Know

Miss Jarrett, the math teacher, arrives at Keenan's party with a surprise. She gives everyone an invitation of her own. Look at Miss Jarrett's invitation, break the code, and find the time of the contest.

Code-Breakers Contest

Date: February 6

Where: At the School

Time: 6^2-5^2 o'clock

1. One student guessed 1 o'clock. How do you think he got that answer? Is he correct? Explain how you know.

_____

_____

2. One student guessed 2 o'clock. How do you think she got that answer? Is she correct? How do you know?

_____

_____

3. Make your own guess, then check your answer. What time will the contest start? Show your work.

4. Do you think it will be during daytime or at night? Explain your answer.

_____

5. The address of Keenan's school is $40^2 - 99$ Cherry Street. What is the address number? Make a guess first. Then find the solution. Show your work.

Lesson 2 Write a Plan

Kirstie asked Keenan to tell her how many people would be at the math party. Keenan answered, "I'm expecting the number of people, including myself, to be the square root of 169." How many people will be at Keenan's math party?

Write a plan to solve the problem.

Step 1   Write in your own words what you need to find out.

_____

_____

_____

Step 2   Write the facts that will be useful.

_____

_____

_____

Step 3   Explain or show how you will solve the problem.

_____

_____

_____

_____

_____

_____

_____

_____

Guess and Check

Try guessing and checking to solve the problem.

> A *square root* is one of two equal factors of a number. If *S* is the square root of 169, then $169 = S \times S$

Keenan said that the number of people would be the square root of 169. How many people will be at Keenan's math party?

1. Kirstie first guessed 12 as the square root of 169. Was her guess correct? Is the square root of 169 greater than or less than 12? How do you know?

   _____

   _____

2. Next Kirstie guessed 15 as the square root of 169. Was her guess correct? Is the square root of 169 greater than or less than 15? How do you know?

   _____

   _____

3. Now that you have calculated Kirstie's guesses, make your own guess. Then check your answer. How many people will be at Keenan's math party? Show your work.

4. At the math party, more people came than Keenan expected. The number of people turned out to be the square root of 361. How many people actually came to the math party? Show your guesses and your work.

5. The number of adults at the math party will be the square root of 16. How many adults will be there?

   _____

Practice

Here are three practice problems for you.

Quick-Solve 1

Amanda asked Keenan to tell her what time his math party would end. He said, "It will be over when the hour is the square root of 25, plus 30 minutes." What time will the party end?

Quick-Solve 2

Jessie saw this flyer at school. What is the date and time of the math club meeting?

> **Monthly Math Club Meeting**
>
> Topic: The Roots of Math
>
> Date: March $\sqrt{64}$
>
> Time: $\sqrt{16}$ o'clock

Quick-Solve 3

Write your address in exponent form or with a square root. If you have more than one number in your address, you may choose whether to write more than one code. Share your address with a friend to see if they can get the numbers right.

Use What You Know

Look back to page 53 if you need help.

At the math Code-Breakers Contest, each entrant was given a treasure-hunt code. The first clue told them to find room $\sqrt{6{,}724}$. There they would find the next clue. What is the room number they should find?

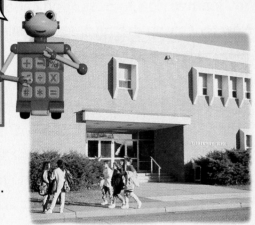

1. Damon's first guess was 50^2. The answer was less than half 6,724. Then he tried 100^2. That answer was too high. What were Damon's first two answers? How did his guesses help him narrow the possibilities?

_____

_____

2. Tanisha looked at the first two digits, 67, to find the closest square roots. She thought, if $8^2 = 64$ and $9^2 = 81$, then the square root of 6,724 must be between 80^2 and 90^2. Explain Tanisha's reasoning. Then calculate 80^2 and 90^2.

_____

_____

_____

3. Tanisha and Amber worked together. Amber reasoned that they should try to square a number half-way between 80 and 90 to further narrow the possibilities. Amber calculated 85^2. What was the result? Was it too high or too low?

_____

4. Now try guessing and checking until you find the square root of 6,724. What is the room number for the first clue of the contest? Show your guesses.

Lesson 3   Solve Multi-Step Problems

You learned how to guess and check to solve problems.
Now try solving this multi-step problem.

Erika found the first room in the Code-Breakers
Contest. There she found an envelope with her name
on it. Inside was the following card. Solve the problems
on the card and help Erika break the code. What is the
room number where she will find her prize?

Congratulations for making it this far! Now write your name
and the value of 66^2 on a card and take it to the teacher in
room $\sqrt{5{,}041}$. Then subtract 6^2 from that room number to
find the room with your prize.

1. What is the number that Erika should write on a card? How do
   you know?

   _____

2. Erika looked at the first two digits of 5,041. She knows that
   $7^2 = 49$, so she tried 70^2 to find a number close to 5,041.
   What was the result? Was this a good guess? Explain.

   _____

   _____

3. Guess and check to find $\sqrt{5{,}041}$. What is the room number
   where a teacher is waiting for Erika's card? Show your work.

4. Now subtract 6^2. What is the room number where Erika will find
   her prize?

   _____

Practice

Here are three practice problems for you.

Quick-Solve 1

Mark's clues were different from Erika's. He had to write his name and 55^2 on a card and take it to room $\sqrt{2,601}$. He then subtracted 4^2 from that room number to find the room with his prize. What number did Mark write on his card? In what room did Mark end up?

Quick-Solve 2

Andrea's clues told her to write 28^2 on a card and take it to room $\sqrt{7,056}$. Then she subtracted 7^2 to find the room with her prize. What number did Andrea write on her card? In what room did she end up?

Quick-Solve 3

Miss Jarrett gave her math students another code to break. Suppose a woman starts a business with 3 employees. Then for 10 years, the number of employees triples each year. Write the number as an exponent with 3 as the base. Then find the number of employees there would be in 10 years.

Use What You Know

Everyone in the Code-Breakers Contest ended up in the same room where there was a huge party! Each person had to break one last code to get in. They had to find the secret passwords. Solve the code puzzle below to find the passwords.

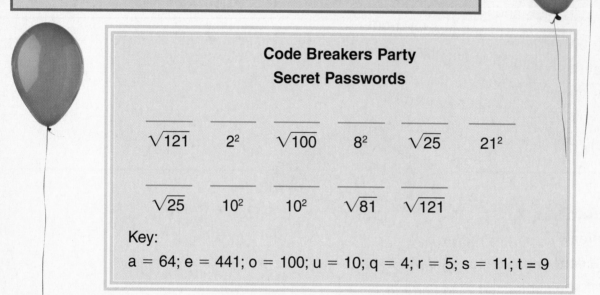

Code Breakers Party
Secret Passwords

___ ___ ___ ___ ___ ___
$\sqrt{121}$ 2^2 $\sqrt{100}$ 8^2 $\sqrt{25}$ 21^2

___ ___ ___ ___ ___
$\sqrt{25}$ 10^2 10^2 $\sqrt{81}$ $\sqrt{121}$

Key:

a = 64; e = 441; o = 100; u = 10; q = 4; r = 5; s = 11; t = 9

1. Find the value of each square root or exponent in the code.

$\sqrt{121}$ = _____ 2^2 = _____ $\sqrt{100}$ = _____

8^2 = _____ $\sqrt{25}$ = _____ 21^2 = _____

10^2 = _____ $\sqrt{81}$ = _____

2. Match the letters in the key to your answers above. What is the first code word? Write it here and in the puzzle.

_____

3. What is the second code word? Note that some of the letters repeat. Write it here and in the puzzle.

_____

4. Now solve one more puzzle, using the key above.

You're a ____ ____ ____ ____!
　　　　 $\sqrt{121}$ $\sqrt{81}$ 8^2 $\sqrt{25}$

Solving Multi-Step Problems: Exponents and Square Roots

Lesson 4   Solve It Your Way

Read each problem and decide how you will find the solution.

You may choose one of these strategies for each problem.

Guess and Check
Solve Multi-Step Problems

1. Jessica invited some friends to come to her house after school. She wrote her address as a code for them, $16^2 + 1$ Oakmont Street. What is Jessica's address?

2. The math class decided to write the address of City Hall as a code. They listed the address as $\sqrt{289}$ Main Street. What is the address of City Hall?

3. Drake asked Sam how many brothers he had. Sam told him that the number of his brothers was $\sqrt{64} - 8$. How many brothers does Sam have?

4. On her next birthday, Veronica's age will be a number that is the square of a one-digit number. Veronica is a teenager. How old will she be on her birthday?

5. Break the code and find the secret word.

    _____ _____ _____ _____

    $\sqrt{169}$ $\sqrt{121}$ $\sqrt{324}$ $\sqrt{289}$

    Key: a = 11
          h = 17
          m = 13
          t = 18

6. Break the code and find the secret word.

    _____ _____ _____ _____

    15^2 14^2 19^2 16^2

    Key: c = 225
          d = 361
          e = 256
          o = 196

Application: Choosing a Strategy

59

Practice

Now write your own problems using exponents and square roots.

Quick-Solve 1

The answer to a problem is 21. What might the question be? Write your own problem to share with a friend. If your friend does not get an answer of 21, discuss how you might change the problem or the solution to match.

Quick-Solve 2

The answer to a problem is $\sqrt{529}$. What might the question be? Write your own problem to share with a friend. If your friend does not get an answer of $\sqrt{529}$, discuss how you might change the problem or the solution to match.

Quick-Solve 3

The answer to a problem is $6^2 + 2$. What might the question be? Write your own problem to share with a friend. If your friend does not get an answer of $6^2 + 2$, discuss how you might change the problem or the solution to match.

Review   Show What You Know

Work in a small group. Write your own secret codes from the key below. Then share your codes with a friend.

Key:

Numbers that have been squared:

a = 4	e = 9	i = 16	o = 25	u = 36
b = 49	c = 64	d = 81	f = 100	g = 121

Numbers that are square roots:

h = 2	k = 3	l = 5	m = 6	n = 7
p = 8	r = 10	s = 11	t = 12	w = 13

1. Begin with a single word. Use at least 4 letters. Write the clues as a number squared or as a square root. For example, if you want to use an *a,* the clue might be 2^2.

   _____   _____   _____   _____

   Clues:

2. Now write your own coded message. If you need letters that are not included in the key, make up your own key for those letters. Share your coded message with others to see if they can break the code.

Read each problem and decide how you will find the solution.

You can choose from all these strategies!

Make a Model
Use a Formula
Guess and Check
Solve Multi-Step Problems

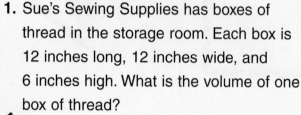

1. Sue's Sewing Supplies has boxes of thread in the storage room. Each box is 12 inches long, 12 inches wide, and 6 inches high. What is the volume of one box of thread?

2. Box A is 6 cm long and 4 cm wide. Box B is 5 cm long and 6 cm wide. Both boxes have a volume of 120 cubic centimeters. Which box has the greater height?

3. A net for a rectangular box is drawn on the graph paper below. Find the surface area of the box.

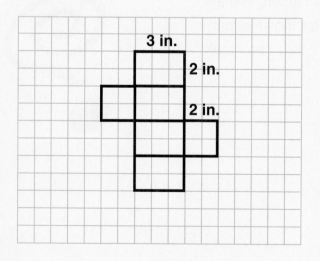

3 in.
2 in.
2 in.

4. A net for a rectangular box is drawn on the graph paper below. Find the surface area of the box.

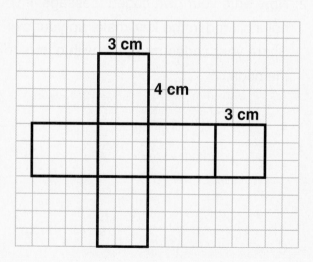

3 cm
4 cm
3 cm

5. Look at the drawing below. Is it a net? Write *yes* or *no*.

6. Look at the drawing below. Is it a net? Write *yes* or *no*.

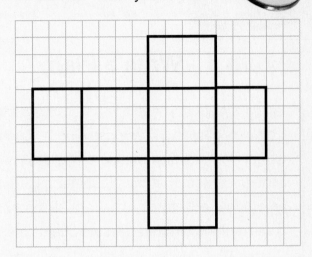

7. Michelle had a party for her math class. She listed her address on the invitation as 71^2 Macon Avenue. Then she listed her telephone number as $355 - 68^2$. What is Michelle's address? What is her telephone number?

8. Ms. Sorrell gave a group of students a treasure map. It told them to start at the old oak tree and take $\sqrt{324}$ steps east. Then they are to turn and take 4^2 steps north. How many steps east should they take? How many steps north should they take?

9. Break the square-root code and find the secret word.

$$\overline{\hspace{1.2cm}} \quad \overline{\hspace{1.2cm}} \quad \overline{\hspace{1.2cm}} \quad \overline{\hspace{1.2cm}} \quad \overline{\hspace{1.2cm}}$$
$$\sqrt{400} \quad \sqrt{576} \quad \sqrt{144} \quad \sqrt{225} \quad \sqrt{225}$$

Key: e = 12
         g = 20
         s = 15
         u = 24

10. Break the code of squares and find the secret word.

$$\overline{\hspace{1.2cm}} \quad \overline{\hspace{1.2cm}} \quad \overline{\hspace{1.2cm}} \quad \overline{\hspace{1.2cm}} \quad \overline{\hspace{1.2cm}}$$
$$11^2 \quad 17^2 \quad 18^2 \quad 11^2 \quad 13^2$$

Key: c = 121
         e = 324
         h = 289
         k = 169

UNIT 5 Games and Contests

Lesson 1   Write a Plan

Logan is playing *Wilderness Quest,* a computer game. He must first choose a character, and then choose an item that the character might use on an outdoor adventure. What are all the possible combinations of characters and items?

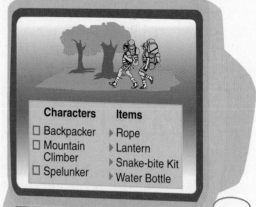

Characters
- ☐ Backpacker
- ☐ Mountain Climber
- ☐ Spelunker

Items
- ▸ Rope
- ▸ Lantern
- ▸ Snake-bite Kit
- ▸ Water Bottle

Write a plan to solve the problem.

Step 1   Write in your own words what you need to find out.

_____

_____

Step 2   Write the facts that will be useful.

_____

_____

Step 3   Explain or show how you will solve the problem.

_____

_____

_____

_____

_____

_____

_____

_____

Writing a Plan: Data and Probability

Make a Tree Diagram

Remember: 1 of 4 = $\frac{1}{4}$

Try making a tree diagram to show the possible combinations.

> To find all the possible combinations, draw a tree diagram. How many possible combinations of characters and items can Logan choose from?

1. Fill in the information in the tree diagram. The first one is done for you.

Characters	Items	Combinations
Backpacker	Rope	Backpacker, Rope
	Lantern	Backpacker, Lantern
	Snake-bite Kit	Backpacker, Snake-bite Kit
	Water Bottle	Backpacker, Water Bottle
Mountain Climber		
Spelunker		

2. Of all the possible characters, what is the probability of Logan choosing the Spelunker? P(Spelunker) = _____ of _____ = _____

3. How many different combinations of characters and items are possible? _____

4. Write a ratio to show the probability that Logan will choose the Backpacker and the Snake-bite Kit. P(Backpacker, Snake-bite Kit) = _____

Practice

Here are three practice problems for you.

Spacecraft	Equipment
☐ Unmanned Probe	▶ Radar
☐ Manned Rocket	▶ Communication Laser
	▶ Radiation Meter

Quick-Solve 1

Tanya enjoys playing *Blast Off!*, a space exploration computer game. Tanya must choose the type of spacecraft and equipment to place on the craft. Draw a tree diagram. What are all the possible combinations of spacecraft and equipment?

Quick-Solve 2

Tanya chooses an Unmanned Probe as her spacecraft to visit a planet. What is the probability that she will choose a Radiation Meter for her equipment?

Quick-Solve 3

The game allows Tanya to choose from among these 3 planets: Mars, Jupiter, and Saturn. What is the probability of choosing a Manned Rocket equipped with a Communication Laser going to Jupiter? How do you know?

Use What You Know

Amelia is playing the computer game *Treasure Hunt.*
She dives into the sea and finds two shipwrecks that
each contain 3 locked treasure chests. Only one
chest from each shipwreck can be brought to the
surface. Amelia will win if she can bring up treasure
worth exactly 70 points. What is the probability
that Amelia will win the game?

Items in the treasure chests and their value are
listed below. Make a tree diagram to find all of
the possible combinations. Then find the total
points of the items from the treasure chests.

1. Make a tree diagram to show all the possible combinations and their point totals.

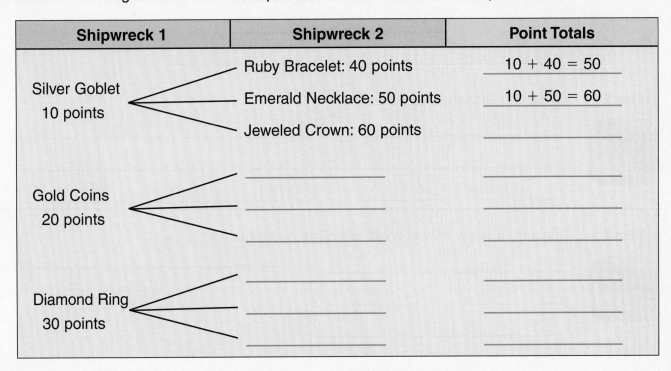

Shipwreck 1	Shipwreck 2	Point Totals
Silver Goblet 10 points	Ruby Bracelet: 40 points	10 + 40 = 50
	Emerald Necklace: 50 points	10 + 50 = 60
	Jeweled Crown: 60 points	
Gold Coins 20 points		
Diamond Ring 30 points		

2. How many different combinations of treasure from the 2 shipwrecks

are possible? _____

3. What is the probability that Amelia will win the game? _____

How do you know? _____

Making a Tree Diagram: Data and Probability

Lesson 2   Write a Plan

Hamburger Heaven is having a contest. Without looking, customers draw tokens from three jars, one labeled "Hamburger," another labeled "Fries," and the other, "Shake." Each token is either red or blue. If a customer picks 2 or more red tokens, he or she will receive a discount on the next meal. What is the probability of winning a discount?

Hamburger Heaven
★ Contest ★
Draw tokens to win a
25% Discount
on your next meal!

Write a plan to solve the problem.

Step 1   Write in your own words what you need to find out.

_____

_____

_____

Step 2   Write the facts that will be useful.

_____

_____

_____

Step 3   Explain or show how you will solve the problem.

_____

_____

_____

_____

_____

_____

_____

Make a Tree Diagram

Try making a tree diagram to solve the problem.

To find all the possible combinations, draw a tree diagram. What is the probability of winning a discount?

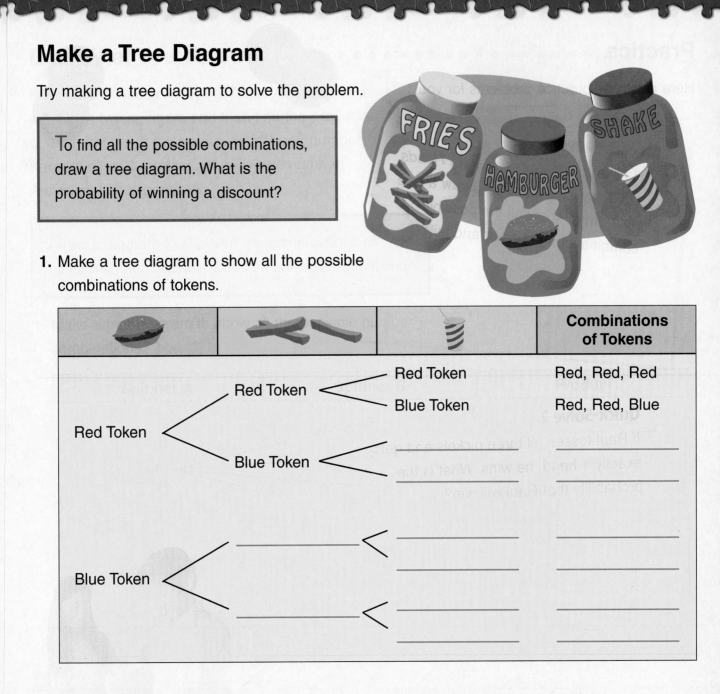

1. Make a tree diagram to show all the possible combinations of tokens.

			Combinations of Tokens
Red Token — Red Token — Red Token	Red, Red, Red
		Blue Token	Red, Red, Blue
	Blue Token		
Blue Token			

2. How many different combinations of tokens are possible? _____

3. What is the probability of winning a discount? How do you know?

_____

4. A customer can win a free drink by drawing a red Hamburger token, a blue Fries token, and a Shake token of either color. What is the

   probability of earning a free drink? _____

Practice

Now write your own problems.

Quick-Solve 1

The answer to a problem is "The number of possible outcomes is 12." What might the question be? Write your own problem to share with a friend. If your friend does not get the same answer, discuss how you might change the problem or the solution to match.

Quick-Solve 2

The answer to a problem is "The probability is $\frac{1}{4}$." What might the question be? Write your own problem to share with a friend. If your friend does not get the same answer, discuss how you might change the problem or the solution to match.

Quick-Solve 3

The answer to a problem is "The game is fair." What might the question be? Write your own problem to share with a friend. If your friend does not get the same answer, discuss how you might change the problem or the solution to match.

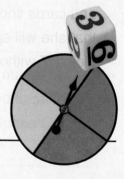

Applying Strategies

Work with a partner. You will need a coin and a number cube. Make three index cards with a triangle, a square, and a circle drawn on them. You will also need a spinner with 5 sections colored blue, red, yellow, orange and green.

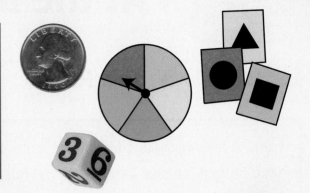

Draw a tree diagram or make a table for each experiment.

1. Toss the coin. Toss the cube. What are the possible outcomes?

2. Toss the coin. Spin the spinner. Pick a card. What is the chance that you tossed heads, spun yellow, and picked the square?

3. Make up your own game using at least three of the objects. Write your own rules. Does everyone have an equal chance to win?

UNIT 6 At the Mall

Lesson 1   Write a Plan

Pam, Alan, Alexis, and Mike went to the mall to buy T-shirts. Mike bought the star T-shirt. Pam did not buy the soccer shirt. Pam told Alan that she liked his sun T-shirt. Alexis did not buy the holiday T-shirt. Who bought each shirt?

Write a plan to solve the problem.

Step 1   Write in your own words what you need to find out.

_____

_____

_____

Step 2   Write the facts that will be useful.

_____

_____

_____

Step 3   Explain or show how you will solve the problem.

_____

_____

_____

_____

_____

_____

_____

Writing a Plan: Comparing Data

Use Logical Reasoning

Try using logical reasoning to solve the problem.

> **Sometimes a table can help you to compare data.**

> **R**ead each clue in the problem on page 78. Decide whether to write *yes* or *no* in each box of the table. Who bought each T-shirt?

Shirts Bought at the Mall

	Star	Soccer	Sun	Holiday
Pam				
Alan				
Alexis				
Mike				

1. The first clue provides specific information about the shirt that Mike bought. Write *yes* in the table to indicate Mike's choice. You can then fill in 6 spaces with *no.* Explain the reason why those spaces can be filled in from this clue.

_____

_____

2. Look at the clues to find another definite answer. It is logical to guess what shirt Alan bought. Fill in the table with *yes* or *no* to indicate his choice and what cannot be true.

3. Now you can complete the table for the choices made by Pam and Alexis. How do you know what they bought?

_____

_____

4. Who bought each shirt?

Star _____   Soccer _____

Sun _____   Holiday _____

Practice

Here are three practice problems for you.

Quick-Solve 1

At the food court, Nick, Mia, and Andy each ordered a slice of pizza. One had pepperoni, one had mushroom, and one had cheese only. Andy does not like mushrooms. Mia does not like mushrooms or pepperoni. Who ordered each slice of pizza?

	Pepperoni	Mushroom	Cheese
Nick			
Mia			
Andy			

Quick-Solve 2

After shopping, Sue, Joe, and Josh checked to see how much money they each had left. One had $5.25, one had $10.50, and one had $16.00. Sue had more than $10.00. Joe had 7 bills. How much money did each person have left?

	$5.25	$10.50	$16.00
Sue			
Joe			
Josh			

Quick-Solve 3

Four of the stores in the mall are numbered 18, 24, 27, and 32. One sells picture frames, one sells clothes, one sells sewing supplies, and one sells videos. The frame store's number is a multiple of 6. The clothing store's number is not an odd number. The sewing store's number is divisible by 9 and by 2. The video store's number is not an even number. What is the number for each store?

	18	24	27	32
Frames				
Clothes				
Sewing				
Videos				

Use What You Know

Look back to page 79 if you need help.

Miranda, Peter, Maura, and Ed each bought different items. One bought shoes, one bought a book, one bought a shirt, and one bought a card. Miranda did not buy a book. Ed did not need new shoes. Maura wanted to buy Peter a birthday card. Ed asked Peter if he could borrow the book he bought. What did each person buy?

Shopping Items

	Shoes	Book	Shirt	Card
Miranda				
Peter				
Maura				
Ed				

1. Read the problem to look for a definite answer given. You should know what Maura bought. Write *yes* in the table to indicate her choice. Explain how this single clue helps you to fill in other boxes in the table.

_____

_____

2. Look at the clues to find another definite answer. It is logical to guess what Peter bought. Fill in the table with *yes* or *no* to indicate his choice and what cannot be true.

3. Now you can complete the table for the choices made by Miranda and Ed. How do you know what they bought?

_____

4. What did each person buy?

Miranda _____   Peter _____

Maura _____   Ed _____

Lesson 2 Write a Plan

Friends for All is a group that brings students and senior adults together. Last month, *Friends for All* went to the mall. The Venn diagram shows how many members of the group went into different stores. How many members went into all three stores?

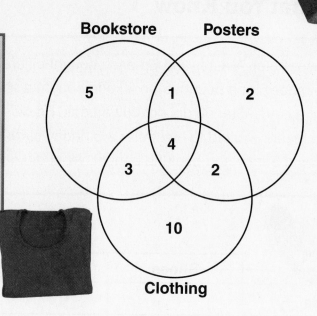

Bookstore   **Posters**

5   1   2

4

3   2

10

Clothing

Write a plan to solve the problem.

Step 1

Write in your own words what you need to find out.

_____

_____

_____

Step 2

Write the facts that will be useful.

_____

_____

_____

Step 3

Explain or show how you will solve the problem.

_____

_____

_____

_____

_____

_____

_____

Use Logical Reasoning

Try using logical reasoning to solve the problem.

> Use different colors to shade each circle of the Venn diagram. Then look at the part of the diagram that is shaded by all three colors. How many members went into all three stores?

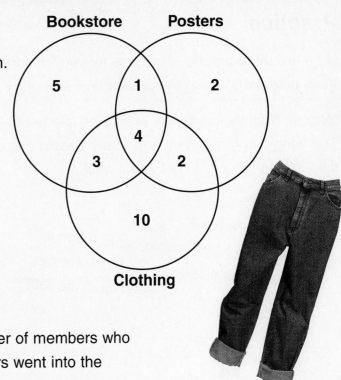

Bookstore   **Posters**

5   1   2

4

3   2

10

Clothing

1. Color yellow the circle that shows the number of members who went into the bookstore. How many members went into the bookstore? How do you know?

_____

2. Color blue the circle that shows the number of members who went into the poster store. How many members went into the poster store? How do you know?

_____

3. Look at the part of the Venn diagram that is shaded both yellow and blue. What information does that tell you about the people represented by the numbers?

_____

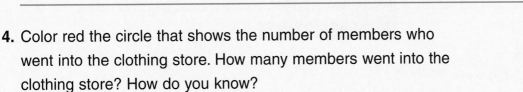

4. Color red the circle that shows the number of members who went into the clothing store. How many members went into the clothing store? How do you know?

_____

5. Look at the part of the Venn diagram that is shaded red, yellow, and blue. How many members went into all three stores? How do you know?

_____

Practice

Here are three practice problems for you. Use the Venn diagram to solve the problems.

Monster Mall took a survey of how people get to the mall. The Venn diagram shows how many people use buses, cars, or the subway to get to the mall.

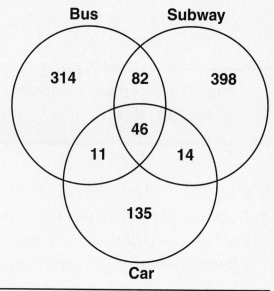

Quick-Solve 1

A total of 206 people get to the mall using the same way as Mrs. Alvarez. How does Mrs. Alvarez get to the mall?

Quick-Solve 2

Look at 82, 11, 14, and 46 on the Venn diagram. Those numbers represent people who use more than one means of transportation to get to the mall. What is true of the people represented by 46 that is not true of the others?

Quick-Solve 3

How many people were surveyed in all? How many people use a single means of transportation to get to the mall?

Use What You Know

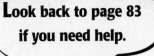
Look back to page 83 if you need help.

> A bus carrying a tour group stops for a one-hour break at Monster Mall. The Venn diagram shows the number of people from the tour bus that visit different places in the mall. How many of them go to three places?

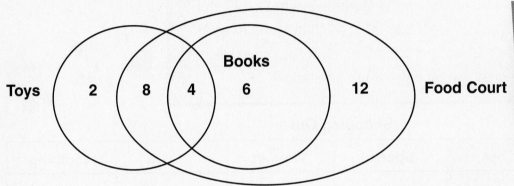

Books

Toys 2 8 4 6 12 **Food Court**

1. There are 40 people on the tour bus. How many of them do not go into the mall? How do you know?

_____

2. Color blue the oval that shows the number of people who visit the food court. How many people go into the food court? How many people do not go into the food court?

_____

3. How many people visit the toy store or the bookstore, but not both? How do you know?

_____

4. How many people from the tour bus visit three places in Monster Mall during their break?

_____

5. What fraction represents the number of people who went to the food court and the toy store, but not the bookstore?

_____

Lesson 3   Work Backward

You have used logical reasoning to solve problems.
Now try working backward to solve problems.

When Mr. Adams finished buying four items at four different stores,
he had $4.00 left. He spent $18.41 on the fourth item, but he was
not in the sports store or vitamin store. He went to the music store
second and spent $17.80. In the sports store he spent $21.47, but
he did not go there first. He spent $30.32 in the first store. In what
order did Mr. Adams go to the stores? What did he spend in each
place? How much money did he have when he started?

Shopping Order

Order	Cost	Sports	Vitamin	Music	Clothing
First					
Second					
Third					
Fourth					

1. Read the problem to look for a definite answer given. Write *yes*
   in the table to indicate which store was second. Write the amount
   spent there. Be sure to write *no* in the places where you can.

2. Complete the table. In what order did Mr. Adams go to the stores?
   List them from first to fourth.

_____

3. What did Mr. Adams spend in each place?

   Sports _____   Vitamin _____

   Music _____   Clothing _____

4. If he had $4.00 left, how much money did Mr. Adams have when
   he started? Show your work.

Working Backward: Comparing Data

Practice

Here are three practice problems for you.

Quick-Solve 1

Chad got on the elevator in the mall at the first floor. At the second floor, 3 people got off and 7 people got on. At the third floor, 8 people got off and 4 people got on. When he got off on the fourth floor, 5 people exited with him, leaving the elevator empty. How many people got on the elevator with Chad at the first floor?

Quick-Solve 2

Caroline had $4.58 left after she finished shopping. In one store, she spent $20.75 on a shirt. In another store, she returned some shoes and received a refund of $27.81. In the last store she entered, she spent $32.48 on a pair of skates. How much money did Caroline have when she started shopping?

Quick-Solve 3

Sheena is getting ready for a marathon race. She ran 10 miles today. She didn't run very far the first day, but the second day she ran twice as far. The third day, she was able to run the distance of the first two days added together. Today she ran 1 more mile than yesterday. How far did Sheena run the first day?

Use What You Know

Tanya conducted a survey of 100 people at the mall. She named three ice cream flavors and asked participants to tell if they like one, two, or all three of them. Each single flavor got the same number of votes. Two of the 2-choice combinations each received 11 votes. The number of people who voted for all three flavors was 42. Half that number voted for Pecan Praline and Rocky Road. How many people voted for only Peppermint?

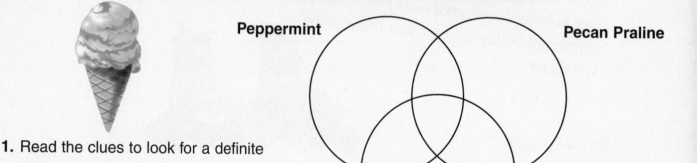

Peppermint   **Pecan Praline**

Rocky Road

1. Read the clues to look for a definite answer given. Write the number in the part of the Venn diagram that shows all three flavors were selected.

2. How many people voted for Rocky Road and Pecan Praline? How do you know? Write the number in the diagram.

_____

_____

3. Complete the Venn diagram to show all of the survey results. How many people voted for only Peppermint? How do you know?

_____

_____

4. How many people were surveyed who did not like Pecan Praline? How do you know?

_____

_____

Lesson 4 Solve It Your Way

Read each problem and decide how you will find the solution.

You may choose one of these strategies for each problem.

Use Logical Reasoning
Work Backward

1. Samantha, Glen, April, and Adam bought four different items at the mall. They spent $1.09, $5.52, $9.44, and $12.76. Samantha did not spend the most or the least. Adam was with the girl who spent the least. Glen spent less than Samantha and Adam. Who spent each amount?

	$1.09	$5.52	$9.44	$12.76
Samantha				
Glen				
April				
Adam				

2. Jerry, Helen, Carlton, and Raymond work in the mall. Each of them sells something different: ice cream, clothing, shoes, and pretzels. Raymond wears what he sells. Carlton and Helen eat what they sell, but Helen does not sell anything cold. Jerry sells only pairs of items. What does each of them sell?

	Ice Cream	Clothing	Shoes	Pretzels
Jerry				
Helen				
Carlton				
Raymond				

Practice

Now write your own problems using logic or working backward.

Quick-Solve 1

The answer to a problem is "Jill sells computers." What might the question be? Write your own problem to share with a friend. If your friend does not get an answer that matches Jill with computers, discuss how you might change the problem or the clues.

Quick-Solve 2

The answer to a problem is "15 people travel to work in cars." What might the question be? Write your own problem to share with a friend. If your friend does not get an answer of 15 people in cars, discuss how you might change the problem or the clues.

Quick-Solve 3

The answer to a problem is "Mr. Payton had $50.00 when he started shopping." What might the question be? Write your own problem to share with a friend. If your friend does not get an answer that matches Mr. Payton with $50.00, discuss how you might change the problem or the clues.

Work in a group to conduct your own survey.

Choose three types of fun activities for your survey. Try to be specific, such as *riding a bicycle, ice skating,* and *playing baseball.* Ask at least 10 people to vote on activities they like to do. You may want to record votes with tally marks first and then add the numbers. Show the results of your survey in a Venn diagram.

Favorite Activities

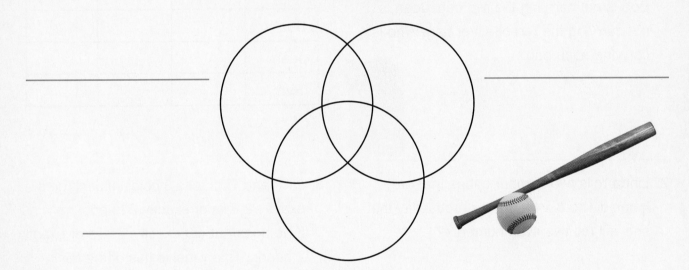

1. What activities did you choose? Write them here and on the Venn diagram.

_____

2. How many people did you survey? _____

3. If nobody voted for a particular activity or a combination, how would you show that in the Venn diagram?

_____

4. Complete your Venn diagram. How many people

voted for all three of the activities that you chose? _____

Extension: Communicating Mathematically

Read each problem and decide how you will find the solution.

Wow! You can choose from all these strategies!

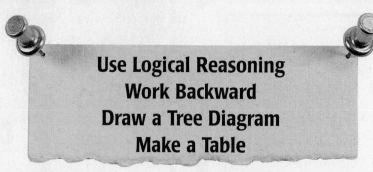

**Use Logical Reasoning
Work Backward
Draw a Tree Diagram
Make a Table**

1. Three friends each have a shopping bag. One is red, one is brown, and one is silver. Bob is not carrying the red bag, Jean is not carrying the red or silver bag. Who is carrying each bag?

	Red	Brown	Silver
Bob			
Jean			
Tom			

2. Linda rolls two number cubes that are labeled 1 to 6. What is the probability that she will roll two even numbers?

3. Jack and Tina toss 3 coins. If Jack gets exactly 2 tails or exactly 2 heads, he wins. If he does not get exactly 2 tails or exactly 2 heads, Tina wins. Is this game fair?

4. Adam, Deb, Nathan, and Rina play different sports. Adam doesn't play baseball. Nathan doesn't play soccer. Deb has a soccer match on Saturday. Rina is going to watch Nathan play football. Who plays each sport?

	Basketball	Baseball	Soccer	Football
Adam				
Deb				
Nathan				
Rina				

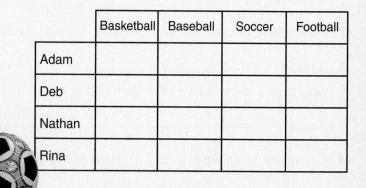

5. Paul invited friends over for pizza and a movie. After shopping, he had $9.56 left. He bought two extra-large pizzas for $29.25. He spent $6.50 on three large bottles of soft drinks. At the movie rental store, he paid $3.99. How much money did Paul have to spend on his party?

6. Jill and Mark board an empty bus to go to Paul's house. Some people get on the bus at the first stop. At the second bus stop, 7 people get off and 5 people get on. At the third stop, 15 people get off and 8 get on. At the last stop, 9 people get off with Jill and Mark, leaving the bus empty. How many people got on the bus at the first stop?

7. Wendy and Brian play a game with 2 spinners. They spin both spinners and then find the product of the numbers. If Wendy spins a product of 6, she will win. If Brian spins a product of 12, he will win. Who is most likely to win?

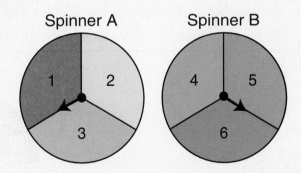

Spinner A

Spinner B

Final Review

Read each problem. Then Solve.

Wow! Now you can choose from all these strategies!

Choose the Operation   **Solve Multi-Step Problems**
Make a Graph   **Make an Organized List**
Make a Model   **Use a Formula**
Guess and Check   **Make a Table**
Make a Tree Diagram   **Work Backward**
Use Logical Reasoning

1. A pet store is having a 30% off sale. If a large dog bowl is regularly priced at $5.49, how much will it cost on sale? Round your answer to the nearest cent.

2. At the pet store, doghouses and crates are on sale for 25% off. How much will it cost on sale for a $91.99 doghouse and a $54.59 crate? Round your answer to the nearest cent.

3. Ron buys 2 cat toys that cost $2.58 each. He also buys a cat bed that is $28.99. Tax on his purchase is 7%. What is his total bill?

4. The heights of the starting players of the Chester Middle School basketball team are 66, 68, 69, 67, and 70 inches. What is the mean height of these players?

5. The weights of the starting players of the Jackson Middle School basketball team are 120, 122, 129, 122, and 123 pounds. What is the mode of the weight of these players?

6. The heights of the starting players of the Chester High School basketball team are 68, 69, 71, 72, and 73 inches. What is the median height of these players?

94

Cumulative Review: Applying Strategies

7. Fatima made a clay bowl for her father. She put it in a box that was 12 inches wide, 12 inches long, and 9 inches high. What was the volume of that box?

8. Ivan has a small box where he keeps his rock collection. It is 14 inches long, 8 inches wide, and 3 inches high. What is the volume of Ivan's box?

9. A net for a rectangular box is drawn on the graph paper below. Find the surface area of the box.

3 cm

3 cm

3 cm

10. Look at the drawing below. Is it a net? Write *yes* or *no*.

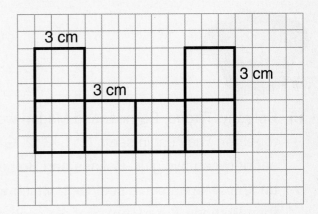

3 cm

3 cm

3 cm

11. Break the code of squares and find the secret word.

_____ _____ _____ _____ _____
21^2 10^2 19^2 12^2 15^2

Key: c = 144
      i = 361
      k = 225
      q = 441
      u = 100

12. Break the square root code and find the secret word.

_____ _____ _____ _____ _____
$\sqrt{625}$ $\sqrt{529}$ $\sqrt{729}$ $\sqrt{324}$ $\sqrt{484}$

Key: e = 22
      l = 27
      o = 23
      s = 25
      v = 18

13. Jacksonville's school cafeteria sells muffins, eggs, and pancakes for breakfast. It also sells orange juice and milk. If a student chooses one drink and one food item, how many combination choices does he or she have for breakfast?

14. Carrie is playing a game with the spinner and cards shown. What is the probability that she will spin an even number and pick an *N*?

15. Bethany, Tyrone, Belinda, and Megan went to see a play together. They sat in seats G11, G12, G13, and G14. Tyrone sat between two girls. Belinda and Bethany sat beside one another. Megan sat in seat G11, which was nearer Belinda than Bethany. From what seat did each person watch the play? Hint: Begin with the last clue and work backward.

Theater Seats

Seat	Bethany	Tyrone	Belinda	Megan
G11				
G12				
G13				
G14				

16. Is it possible that Megan and Belinda sat beside one another? Explain why or why not.

_____

_____